Writing My Way Home

poems by

Linda Recco O'Connell

Writing My Way Home

Text © Linda Recco O'Connell
www.facebook.com/LindaReccoOConnellPoetry

Back cover photo © John Hardesty

Design/Art Direction Lisa Breslow Thompson
LisaThompsonGraphicDesign.com

Library of Congress Control Number: 2019914524
ISBN: 9781941573211

Published by Damianos Publishing
Saxonville Mills
1630 Concord Street
Framingham, MA 01701
www.DamianosPublishing.com

Produced through Silver Street Media by Bridgeport National Bindery, Agawam, MA USA

First printed 2019

Dedication

*To my babies in heaven
who allowed the first words
to emerge from my heart.
I still think of you.*

Gratitude

*With loving thanks to my husband Mike
and my two sons, Michael and Nicholas.*

And, also, my parents John and Carol Recco.

*To Mark Pearce who encouraged me from the beginning.
And for the life changing day at The Montserrat Poetry
Festival. You gave me confidence I never knew I had.*

*To all the warm, yellow dogs who sat by my side
and listened.*

Contents

Muse

Once, in the beginning
as I was leaving
she reached out and
fed me a piece of raw fennel –
Its hard anise crunch,
clean and so unexpected –
I wanted to thrive in that moment;
tuck myself into a book of love poems
and furrow in between the 3rd and 4th stanza –
and be the one line
that one breath of fresh air –
that made the poem worthy.

Passing by Hunnewell Farm

The air spiked with honey,
barn red wood, leaves the color of caraway seeds.

Gray stones snap under my leather boots
as I walk towards the fence.

I press my eye against the camera, capture the breeze
drift through the tall grass
the cow is grazing.

The innocence of this animal,
moseying toward the warmth
of the sun
this October morning.

Cows
(after reading Tulips by A. E. Stallings)

The cows make me want to smile
something about the way they clomp
from side to side carrying their bodies' heavy load
just one behind another single file.

The cows kind of make me feel lonely
something about the way they walk
never losing their composure
like regimented soldiers almost holy.

The cows somehow warm my heart
something about the way
they parade in the mud
a mindful and obedient work of art!

Tonight

Tonight, I will sit beside the moon

dangle my legs

over the edge,

find the perfect words

and try to write a verse.

I'll grab my pen

and probably

write about love again.

Would They Know?

If I left this world today would they even know
I love buttercups in a summer field held under my chin.
And I don't even like butter?

Would they even know I love the smell of roasting chicken
On a winter's day because it reminds me
Of the great childhood I had?

Would they even know I was in love with Paul McCartney
    of the Beatles
And I swore he was in love with me.
And that I practiced kissing his lips on the album cover?

Would they even know if I smile at a stranger
And he smiles back,
It warms my heart for an entire month?

Would they even know I lay awake at night
And send blessings to every person I love
Just because it makes me feel good?

Would they even know I married my husband
The truest of true gentleman,
Because he reminded me of my dad?

Would they even know when I walk outside at night
I walk till I find the brightest star then wish upon it
And it twinkles back at me?

Would they even know I don't hate anyone
Not one single person in the whole world
Even if they've been mean to me?

Would they even know when I found poetry
And wrote my first poem I actually found myself
And for the first time I felt whole?

Blessings

Blessings for all things.
For the green beans I snapped in summer on the veranda
with Nana in her little house in Auburndale.
Beans stewing in olive oil, tomatoes and garlic.
And chicken, she would turn into
warming bowls of *Papa soup.*

Blessings for my friend Paula, ten that year
when she spoke to me in line on the first day of school
coaxing me out of my shell.
I won't forget hours on tennis courts and in
swimming pools, sunning our wet skin on hot cement
forever drenched in summer.

And for you my love, blessings for times
in which we came together.
When the sturdiness of your arms around me
and your mouth firm against my forehead was enough.
Forever sure like the truth in our skin.
The way blue skies wear the sun and clouds.

Blessings for my children for being yourselves.
And knowing how to be a friend.
Paying attention when I thought you weren't.
For all your boy humor. (even now)
For one more talk by your bedside.
One more tender hug.

And yes, blessings for my parents.
For a childhood full of light.
For being there for me and my brother.
For not always giving us what we wanted.
And showing me that a marriage
always needs tending to.
Like the perennials in the side yard.

Blessings on all these things and more.
A house with soul. A poem that resonates.
The drunkenness of love.
For branches by a window and figs that taste like honey.
For the sun waiting patiently behind the barn.
And winter mornings that go on forever.

A Small Pot of Pastina ...

stay at home mom;
noun:
1. because no one could love you all day more than me

boils gently on the stove.
The directions say ten minutes.
I watch as the star shaped pasta
yields to the heat of the water.

All day my five year old
and his pals build a fort out of
pine branches and rocks.
I know it's a good day
because they are covered in dirt and grass stains.

Later, that afternoon my eighth grader arrives home.
Starving for dinner after football practice.
He is covered in dirt and grass stains too.

My two boys and the dog hang out
while I whip up something fast to tide them over
before the main meal.
Before dad comes home later from work.

I hear laughter and boy humor in the family room.
I look forward to this time of day.
I peel the cellophane off the orange cheese squares
and lay them on the bottom of the plain white bowls.
The kitchen timer buzzes.

Spooning the pastina into the bowls,
my heart melts along with the cheese
and the small pat of sweet butter.
I see smiles on their faces.

It's just this simple.
Happiness, you know.
I want to remember us this way.
Late October sun pouring through
the screen door.
A bowl of red apples on the table.
Spoonfuls of steaming pasta
rising to our mouths, filling us up
with what remains.

Saturday Morning
for jack

We ate frosted flakes for breakfast
and added more sugar and milk

then settled ourselves on the floor
'Indian style' and turned on The Three Stooges.

He bonked me on the head with his fist, like Moe –
and did that thing
snapping his fingers into his palm
yuh yuh yuh, he snickered

Funny what you remember.
Funny what's endearing –

I like going back inside that tinywide world
shoulder to shoulder with you –
I think it's what they mean by
being present.

It's Like This Mom

This morning I stand in the advancing light
My mind hungry, this world beautiful.

My eyes can't get enough of the cherry trees.
They are so hopeful, so pink.

There's always more I want to say to you.
Writing you a poem makes me feel like a child again.

How do I articulate the world that mothers
embrace us in and love us in.
One that extends for decades and miles.

Those remarkable mother arms
that can soothe anything.
And those mother hands that can iron out any problem
and sew together a family.

I'll always remember sliding into crisp, cool sheets
and you by the side of my bed.
Eskimo and butterfly kisses.
They always come back to me mom.

How beautiful to think of you.
To write about you.
My heart so full from your love.
Blooming like the cherry trees.

My Mother's Perfume

Saturday nights after they left.

I would reach high onto her bureau.

                  A tippy toed ballerina.

Stretching taller, touching, hoping digging deeper.

My hands fumbling the pretty shaped bottles.

And I would imagine me the princess of the ball.

The nights that glittered and sparkled.

Her scent I loved in the air and on my tiny wrists.

And through the gardenias and citrus

                  I felt so loved.

I heard her sing. I saw her comforting smile.

And I would wish someday to be as beautiful.

Momma

Here is my mom.

Standing in Papa's rose garden.

She is holding my brother.

Pregnant with me and days away from delivering.

It's Mother's Day.

I can tell by her corsage.

The garden beds are empty.

But just look at my mother —

All sweetness and light.

The one beautiful

bloom

in the garden that day.

That's Me There

That's me, there
without a care,
perched way up high
just me and my guy
on his broad shoulders
curls wrapped in gold
just smell that beach air
summer breeze blowin' my hair
sunny smile on my face
this world's a lovely place
deep dimpled cheek
just walkin' the beach
shells making a crunch
I love you t...h...i...s much!!! daddy ...
look at that rock
it's shaped just like your heart
pink polka dot suit
was I always that cute?
so happy and free
just my dad and me
I'm so at ease
"Oh daddy, pretty please"
a cookie in hand
gee, life is grand
my prince, my king
with you I sing ...
you are my sunshine!

Not Just Any Man

He says things to me that matter
about life. He's so just nice.
His words are warm all over my face.
Like the sunlight
and the moonlight combined.

He says things to me that matter
about pride. He's my dad.
His words ignite my soul with desire.
Like radiant sparks
into a fire.

He says things to me that matter about love.
He's just so sweet.
And I take it to heart.

He matters to me.

My Father's Handwriting

His broad left hand gripping the pen.
A choke hold.
Crafting letters
half script half print.
With a slight slant.

As unique as his laughter.
As certain as his kindness.

I take stock of the things I've kept.

His parent signature bearing down
on the manilla report card that went back to school.
For sure a visual note to the teacher.
"She will be buckling down" next semester.

His athletic hand
rotating the golf scorecard sideways.
The way lefties do.
Penning pars and birdies
into cramped little squares.

But always.
Always, I return to his letters.
I've saved them all.

The ones that thank me.
The ones that are proud of me.
The ones inscribed in my heart.

I Love You So Much

This is what I saw – an email from my dad,
"Hi Honey" bold print,
written in the entire subject line.
"Fed Ex came, couldn't
wait till Father's Day.
What a surprise!"

He's in his swivel chair in Florida
tapping the phone hard
with his hefty pointer finger.

Light blue cashmere socks
to warm his feet.
Like his every word, the entire paragraph
in that tiny subject line
making me smile
and cry
and warming my heart.

On Approaching Sixty

You can't have it all, but you can have the cherry blossoms
    in spring.
The pink pollen, falling like a February snow.
You can have the sweet breath of a one year old
in the crook of your neck affirming his love.
And God that's so good.

You can have the empathetic yellow dog
with the soulful eyes that assures you
everything will be alright.

And as a parent,
you can have a job well done, having done your best.
You can watch your children become bits and pieces of you
and feel your heart swell with happiness.

You can't have it all but if you look over your shoulder
you can have your Italian grandmother standing next to you
while making tonight's dinner.
Sauce the color of a red sunset.

And seriously you can be thankful for wrinkles at the corners of
    your eyes.
The way they play on your face, the way they add spice and tell
    your story.

You can have that forever friend who you count on
to listen to you, to teach you a serve with a spin, to ace the heck
    of the
doubles team across the net, to knock sense into you until you
    learn about life and love.

And when old age fails you, you can summon the memory of
    that Cape Cod summer.
Feisty little crabs biting your toes. Salt on your tongue and
    cinnamon skin.
Seaweed hula skirts, bologna and mayo on white bread with a
    side of sand.
The juice of a summer peach dripping down your chin and onto
    your throat.

And you can have dreams and love.
Sweet, sweet surrender.
You can kiss the ripe plum of his mouth.
Smell the honeysuckle of his skin, still.

And then there's that voice you can conjure up at will,
like your dad's.
It'll endlessly whisper, you can't have it all
but there is this. And this is what matters.

I Loved You

To the little one ...

I never knew
Or even had to hold
You are in my thoughts so often
My sad story never told.

Tell me, are your eyes
Of blue or maybe olive green?
Is there a curl upon your head?
Sweet baby, I have not seen.

Did you know me well?
For I knew you, little babe of mine
Did you hear me say I love you
Feel my heartbeat all the time?

I never saw your rosebud lips
Or heard your gentle cry
Held your tiny little hand in mine
Sang you a lullaby.

When I arrive in Heaven
I'm sure you'll know it's me
I'll be running towards you
And happy we will be.

The Miscarriages

The miscarriages have no name in this world.

They are all alone, faraway and unreachable.

No one to love and care for them

or sing them a song.

They are left to do this on their own.

Never an identity had
or anything in common with
life or death.

No mark of a human touch
or footprint in the snow.

Just stillness all around.

Just a silent voice echoing
in my mind.

Nana

Bear with me.
I want to get it right.

The first floor of a two family house.
The cramped kitchen.
The white porcelain stove
 lit with a match.

The aluminum pot.
Stacked with tomatoes and meat bones.
Let me tell you.
No ordinary sauce.

Nana, with her shy smile and
her auburn hair.
Her broken English.
Words barely heard anymore.

She returns to me in the
fading black and white picture.

Her strong hand stirring.
Stirring the mixture with the wooden spoon.

Now I ache when I find her.

She is more alive
than the apple tree blooming outside.

More lasting
than my own smile.
Spreading like butter across my face.

At The Bus Station

When the girl got off the bus in the college town,
she leapt up and wrapped her legs around the waist
of the boy she'd come to visit,
and they spun
around and around, embracing and shrieking with joy.
Their love prodded the sun out from behind the cumulous
cloud.

That was decades ago.

Now, I see you every day.

We eat meals together on plates from the *Jack and Jill* shower.

But when we lie in bed at night, I still feel your eyes on me,
        moonstruck.
And when your hand wraps around my hand
I feel the link that has formed us,
tighten.

Things I Never Knew I Loved
(after Nazim Hikmet)

Fifteen years old. I'm sitting by the phone in the kitchen.
It's 4:30 in late afternoon and the sun is going down.
I never knew I loved the darkness in winter for its recollection
of you.

I never knew I loved the ring of a telephone.
Can someone who doesn't understand how telephones work
love it?
It must be your voice on the other end that I loved;
huddled in the closet with the stretched out cord
asking me out on our first date.

I never knew I loved blizzards
or the Needham High School hill.
And here I've loved snow all this time,
on the inside looking out
as it blankets the pines in our yard.

I never knew I loved a broken leg.
The thick white cast tight up to my knee.
Your perfect penmanship scrolled where I could see it.
I know I don't like hospitals but I did that night.

I always knew I loved the sky.
The way it's rock solid and gentle at the same time.
The way it's always there even when interrupted by clouds.
Even as we chase after it in a climbing plane.

I never knew how much I could learn to love myself
and here you've loved me all this time.
I know all this has been said a thousand times before
and will probably be said again.
I always knew I'd never stop loving you.

I never knew I loved roads.
The smooth ones and even the bumpy ones.
The two of us driving from decade to decade.
The world drifting past us on both sides.
The two of us trusting we'd get through it.

And I know I've always loved trees.
The way they stand the test of time.
Strong, all giving and all seasons never wanting for themselves
anything in return.

I never knew I loved words.
The way they teach and feed me lines.
One word leading another on.
I never knew words could be a gift.

Oh, I just remembered the farms.
I never knew I loved farms.
I never knew how much until now.
I always knew I liked a simple life like ours
basic and just enough.

I always knew I loved the man you are.
The way you loved your mother.
The type of man who is a model for our sons.
The husband you are to me.
And more than anything. More than then. More than now.
This very moment. I always knew I loved your heart.

On My Last Child Leaving Home

Even the thought of it makes me queasy.
Like the first day of the flu.
I swear even my teeth ache.
A kind of fever of my soul.
A chill in my spirit.
A loss of appetite of the female psyche.

Everyone tells me about the empty nest
that I must not look back.
When bowls were filled
with Cheerios and Kraft macaroni and cheese.
And I was teaching how to say thank you's and please.

And Goodnight Moon's pages were pleasantly worn.
And Candy Land and Chutes and Ladders
were the only things that really mattered.

What will become of my butterfly kisses
that tickled your nose?
Who will wish you sweet dreams
and add another blanket when it's cold?

It seems only yesterday you asked me to play Maid Marian
and you'd be Robin Hood.
You said, "I want to marry you mommy"
It was so cute and I understood.

Don't look back they say.
To yesterday.
Back to when the nest
was filled with things like love and kids.

The Empty Nest

Already I feel one of the loose

errant twigs sticking in my side.

The soft fur lining is worn

and the mud has dried.

So has the velvet

of the deep green moss.

Oh, how I am already

feeling this loss.

From The Window

So much sweetness

this house has lived.

Two skinny boys

who barely took up space on earth.

A yellow dog.

And I,

a mother in a breathing poem.

In a stream I love.

The maple blooms.

A Sweet Little Poem

I wanted to write a poem just for you
A sweet little poem
So you'd know how much you mean to me
But you mean too much and the words get jumbled
And I fumble around in my mind
And for days and nights I grope,
For the right phrase
To convey how I feel
But nothing sounds right
For emotions this real

I wanted to write a poem just for you
A sweet little poem
Maybe in Italian so that you would understand then
How much you mean to me
With all those pretty flowing words
Falling off the lips of all those gorgeous girls
Tender words like "come sei bella" and
"La mia stella"
I wanted to write it on sweet smelling pink paper
So even if you read it years later
You'd breathe it in and know it was from me.

I wanted to write a poem just for you
A sweet little poem
To thank you for pulling back all the layers
And how you dug down deep and found me hiding there
That frightened little girl
That I used to be
And how you answered all my unanswered prayers
And set me free

I wanted to write a poem just for you
A sweet little poem
Straight from the very soul of me
That special place I have reserved just for you
Where my heart beats faster than it's ever beaten before
This feeling that is right in the very heart of my chest
These feelings I wanted to be able to express
By writing you a sweet little love poem

36th Anniversary

Didn't we stand there then,
black tuxedo, white dress.
when the world seemed so small?

And oh, the innocence of ours.

The blue soothing sky love in our eyes
and in our hearts.

And weren't we tender,
and awed and scared;
knowing we were stepping from the room of desire
into a lifetime of love?

And wasn't it holy the sweetness of our way?

And were we not simply lovely then?

Were we not as lovely as the white gardenias,
as the moonlit night, as the damp grass on our bare feet?

I think so.

Little Blue

I wrote a few lines from my heart.

And tucked it inside an empty bluebird box.

Now all summer long

as bluebirds flit and glide by,

I hear my words in a song.

Ladybug

Here on six keen legs a life travels

tucked into a tiny red wagon

busy cruising the length of my arm.

She lives in her own perfect world

a life so far from ours

we could only hope to comprehend.

What I see is her poise,

an angel – winged beauty upon rising;

her light rain of luck

all over me.

Simple Pleasures

Very early it's still a bit dark out.
I'm at the porch door with coffee, when
something in the air feels hopeful.

I see the Carolina wren and her mate
scooting up and down and all around –
from tree to tree, to my mail basket making a nest.

He is singing his soothing
teakettle love song
over and over –
"sweet heart sweet heart"

She is sweeping the area
for the tiniest twigs, puffs of my dog's blond fur,
and pine needles.

They are so happy.
They love each other.
They don't notice me.

I think if they could,
they would hug each other.

It's dawn and they are doing their thing together.
She has come close to my window.
I love her chubby chestnut underbelly.
I would like to carefully cup her
in the palm of my hand.

There's just no accounting for the simple pleasures.
How it comes out of nowhere
and bends down,
and kisses your life.

Having A Walk With You
(after Frank O'Hara)

– down to Dunkin Donuts is even more fun
than going to San Miniato or the Loire Valley
or Lucerne
or playing golf at Whistling Straits
in the pouring rain.
Partly because of my love for you,
and partly because of your love for
fire trucks and partly for your love of horses at the barn.
Partly because of the way you smile
and look upside down at me
and sweetly say "Nana"
and partly because you pass nothing by
without loving it much. (the birds, the flags, the dig – digs,)
And partly because you purposely lean over
and say "dog – dog"
to get a wet kiss from Gino.
It's hard to believe when I'm with you
that there can be anything better
in the cool crisp 7 AM mornings in Wellesley –
not the red orange foliage on the maple trees.
Not the sun sneaking up
behind the church steeple.
Not even the smell of fresh coffee.
I look at you, and I would rather look at you
than all the beautiful sites in the world.
Which is why I am telling you this.

For You

So here's a prayer for you if
you ever wake in the night.
As you lie with eyes open or eyes closed,
may something soothe you.
A bluebird,
the smell of the ocean,
the sun on your face,
Raffi's Douglas Mountain,
a kiss –
or even me –
laying awake in my bed
smiling thinking of you.

Nana Linda Day
(for Mike and Nick)

After you leave
the macaroni and cheese
is stuck on the spoon
and the dog is sleeping on top of your blocks
on the floor.
There's a T – Rex in my head
who *r o a r s*
when you're not here.
And yes, I do like 'Bronto' as much as you do.

It's deja vu you know –
in a lifetime ago,
because there's nothing I love more
than to remember my boys like that –
their mouths so full of my name.
Their innocent eyes full of "whys".
Their breath moist
in the curl of my neck –
My whole world.

Putting away the blocks can wait a little longer
not to disturb the dog.
Slowly and deliberately washing the spoon of its cheese,
I glance over my shoulder at Brachiosaurus.
I think he understands.

A Mother's Love
(for Mike and Nick)

I watch him doing something easy,
preparing dinner, lifting his son into the highchair,
and wish that I could ask and he could hear,

but I know now,
that he understands my love
that I have for himself and his brother;
the fullness of it.

The constant.

The beautiful ache in my heart.

Nana, What Is A Poem?

A poem
is when you have summer in your mouth.
It's warm, like fresh blueberries inside a muffin.
And when you taste it
a little smile happens on your face.

A poem
is when you hear
the heartbeat of a tree,
and when words wag their tails.

A poem is what we love and hold inside.
To carry within us, the sky, the clouds,
not only the sun, but the shade.

A poem is a hug with your eyes closed.
It is a feeling,
as if time were nowhere in the background.

Poems are words somersaulting down a hill.

A poem my sweet, I am certain,
is the way I love you.

Why Did the Tree Fall, Nana?

Once there was a tree
a big beautiful tree
who loved the two boys running towards him.
Their arms up high like
limbs in the sky
"look at me, look at me I can fly!"

Oh how he wished he could
run like them
so he called for the wind
and he called for the sun
and he saw the smiles
on the kids having fun

Then this beautiful tree that day
watched us so perfectly happy in our way,
So again he called for the wind
and he called for the sun
and he wanted to smile like the kids having fun.

Oh how he wished
he could run with them-
cuz it's windy and sunny-
and crazy and funny

So he took a deep breath
and he fell and he fell
right onto the house
and onto the flowers –

I think all he wanted
was a love like ours.

Yellow

You have your one darling word
filling you with celebration.

Challenging your innocent tongue.

From mind to mouth
articulating each letter
with precision.

Elongating the yahllll
and the lowwww –

like the drawl of a country love song,
breaking my heart in pieces.

Thrust out your finger at some random entity;
the dog, the lamp, the baby chick
and sing.

This two syllable hue.
Everything is. Everything yellow.

To S.

You are everything real to me
The daylight, the moonlight
and the sugary smell of spring.

You are everything true to me.
The seed, the bud
the blossoms in a meadow, fragrant and pink.

You are everything pure to me.
The bee, the honey
the song in the velvety throat of a bird.

You are everything love to me.
The gentle rain, the red rose,
the lilies of the valley.

Tell me –
How'd you do that?
Plant a garden in the middle of my heart

In The Corner

I'm trying to write something about
this Greek salad with too much oil
in a town with only one gas station.

There's a rip in the orange plastic
in the corner booth where I'm sitting.

I know this because I'm trying to write something
about loneliness.
                About hurting for late afternoon skies in summer.

When sun is thrown against the trees
and the leaves are just about turning.

I'm trying to write something about the passing of time
and how no one knows
what has passed through me.

I write because we move through this world alone.

I'm trying to write about strength because sometimes
I write out of hurt
and how to make hurt okay.

I'm trying to write
because writing might be all we ever have.

And even that might not be enough.

Without Light

can you imagine being so sad

you would get up off the couch

night after night

and lower a pint of ice cream into the well
of your stomach

just so you could feel something down there
tug, at the other end of the rope?

Mean Girls

"Didn't anybody tell ya
Don't go messing with karma
It'll come around" — Brett Dennen

I've put up with you for too long.
You are the wolves in sheep's clothing.
I kept my bruises tucked inside my bones.
I kept giving you another chance.

You are the wolves in sheep's clothing.
You are the women sticking your tongues out.
I kept giving you another chance.
You are the women with barbed wire words.

You are the wolves in sheep's clothing.
I am the woman who isn't taking it anymore.
You are the women sticking your tongues out.
You are the mannequins hiding behind your liquid foundation.

I kept giving you another chance.
I kept my bruises tucked inside my bones.
You are the women with barbed wire words.
I've put up with you far too long.

Dear Mark

The town thinks it's the same without you.

But they're wrong.

The glimmer in the stars aren't even close to what they used be.

It was your eyes that coaxed them out at night.

We were able to touch them; hold one in our bare hand.

And how about the moon?

I can hardly see his face through all that smoldering white and gray.

He seems further away.

The morning dove has lost her voice.

She looks for you.
And because you listened, she so wants to sing!

But it's a different town.
A different old man outside the sandwich shop.

Yet the same kind of lonely, vacant stare.

I happen to know what he's thinking.
He's thinking about a woman standing on a balcony with the
same lonely, vacant stare.

I still don't know what to make of it.

This town.

I'd invent the word absence, if it hadn't already been invented.

I can see you being proud of me.
Using the beat up hammer that you left behind.
I think you left it on purpose so I wouldn't forget you.

How could I ever forget you?

You still drive towards me waving.
In your cream colored van.

In this different town.

To Timmy Fitz

And you, with no shadow now, sleep and be;
deep peace to your bones ...
It is final now,
sleep your untroubled and true dream.
– Antonio Machado

This morning
I am watching the bluebird
amuse himself
sweeping over the grass,
parading into the sky,

of this one world we all belong to –
where everyone and everything
will someday be a part of everything else.

I like to think he was smiling
like I remember you –
your smile, your laugh
drenched in enthusiasm
head thrown back –
all being right with the world
where peace comes free
and easy.

This thought made me feel
for the rest of the morning,
like smiling myself.

Friend

Tonight I am thinking of him.
The sweetness of this man.
Immeasurable as the moon rising,
casting its soft light
on all of us.

How lucky I feel!

I have known
the gentle color of blue.
And I have tasted pure
and simple human love.
I hope he knew how beautiful he was.

For Joe

I sit outside on my front steps
and watch the clouds bloom into white flowers
out of the rooftop across the street.

The warm air moves over my face
like the touch of a friend who knows me.

Far overhead my eyes follow a jet plane
floating through skeleton trees to your place
at the top of the sky, where I will always
see you now.

There's something to say about these moments.

Like last night,
I walked right out onto the planet
and saw your face in the full moon.

That warm borrowed light
was certainly a beautiful thing.

A Conversation With My Dog

Falling in love again I never wanted to, what am I to do
I can't help it"
— Nina Simone

I tell my yellow dog who is lying next to me
about my professor Frank Bidart. He looks
up at me with intent. I love his brown eyes when I talk.
Anybody who knows me, knows I fall in love on a daily
    basis with
all the ordinary mostly. The hard working baristas
downtown, the waiters, the checkout guys at Whole Foods,
Pat Conroy for Prince of Tides, Kate Di Camillo's Because of
    Winn Dixie and the movie that was made from it,
forever Holden Caulfield,
    and the way Keith Whitley sings "Don't Close Your Eyes,"
the little hill town of Assisi Italy,
    the Tin Man because he made my heart hurt *(he already*
    had a heart if you ask me),
an old red barn from afar with an ebony horse peeking out,
people who aren't people collectors.
The underdogs. (my dog nudges my arm to tell him more.)
I say, here I am falling in love again. (which by the way Nina
    Simone sung splendidly)
And now with my teacher, Frank. It's his fault partly. He didn't
    have to be so kind. Or accepting of my answers. "Yes Linda,
    yes yes yes"

That never happened to me before in school.
Listening to him read and talk about Frost
and T.S. Eliot and Lowell

and Gluck (pronounced Glick he told us because of those two
　　　tiny dots above the U)
and my God, Frank O'Hara – I worked my brain into a frenzy.
I wanted to keep my hand up and yell, "Oh Oh Oh I know the
　　　answer" the way the smart kids around me did in Miss
　　　O'Keefe's class.
I say to my dog, how can this be at sixty three? (he stands up and
puts his head in my lap)
I have no fear of the front row now. I never glance at the clock.
　　　Not once.
Whoever said time flies when your'e having fun must have been
　　　in Frank's class. How can 3 hours pass by in one minute?
My dog's eyelids are getting heavy now.
I listen to this Golden breathing –
Air going inside and filling me up like Frank's words in class;
from the half light coming through the window,
and his breath going out.
His one eye opens and looks at me
as if I am his poem.
Exactly how I look adoringly at Frank.
As if he said to me,
"it will all come, if you just wait."

Since Hannah Moved To Maine

I miss you Hannah – Love, Gino

"There's no one in the hood
I don't mean to complain
But I'm not feeling so good
Since Hannah moved to Maine.

Dog bones have no flavor
They all taste so plain
There's no bunny poop to savor
Since Hannah moved to Maine.

No pinecones on the lawn
Not a soul to entertain
All I do is sit and yawn
Since Hannah moved to Maine.

I wonder if she misses me
because I am going insane
I'll just sit here by the tree
Till Hannah comes home from Maine."

Snoop — *everyone's friend*

That's just what life does.
It hits you right smack in the face.
Rips your heart right out of your chest
and throws it into the woods
like an old apple core.

The vet said he was ready
and for us to come in.
He was laying on a pink blanket.
I wondered why they didn't use blue.
He was a boy after all.
"What a good boy!"

God, the way he looked up at me.
The same look he'd give me
when he heard me crying from another room
and he'd come running in to console me.

It was going to be over soon.
He would stop breathing.
That's how I felt.
Like I couldn't breathe.

I just wanted to hold onto him a little longer.
To smell his fur.
To hold his big blocky head in my hands.
And his heart.
Like he held mine.

And thank him for everything.

Thank You

Just around the corner to the elementary school
the late afternoon sun shines brightly through the pines.
And the sweet brown eyes of this friend
sparkle with kindness.

He gladly waits patiently
on the cool green of the grass
to welcome my son and the neighborhood kids.

Before they make the turn towards the house
he hears their laughter, their playfulness.
His sturdy golden body shimmies wildly
and he can hardly contain his happiness.

They are coming.
He humbly cowers down. He loves them.
He paws my son over and over
and smothers him with wet kisses.
All I can hear are little boy giggles.

There's nothing like a dog.
I watch from the garden
with a million smiles in my heart.
I want to freeze this moment.

He scampers so funny
like a squirrel to find a ball,
and comes back with two in his mouth.

The light breeze caresses his soft fur
on that big old head of his.
And dogs don't need to talk.
We hear what they are saying.
We are home.

My Dog Bob

I'll be honest.
I'm emotional when I look back on
their hand drawn pictures of our first dog.
How they felt him in their innocence.

Cray – Pas making them kindergarten artists.
Both choosing Goldenrod, like his sun buttered fur.
It isn't their talent that makes our devoted friend come alive;
for they sweep and stroke wobbly lines;
and smudged details appear to charge their excitement.

Mike depicts him with squiggly sharp claws and long eyelashes.
Nick portrays him with spongy black pads and electric blue eyes.
One is smiling from eyeball to eyeball and composed,
the other resembling a car ride –
head out the window
ears blowing lips flapping.
Flap happy!

I can feel him again.
His heart beats
here on these pages.

Cooper Knew Love
(for Joe)

Even the tiniest heart
can see it coming.

And if he's lucky enough,
It's coming for him.

And for the first time
the sun is up
and the world is warm.

A day of gentle and easy
seems like a year of smiles.

Everything is everything sweet.
This taste of
honey on a tongue.

And it's coming from everyone.

Even the tiniest heart
knows love.

The People Who Work At Peet's Coffee

I wish for you a lifetime of freshly brewed coffee
Italian roast, Sumatra, Arabian Mocha Java
in a warm ceramic cup, with thick frothed 2% milk
and a sprinkle of cinnamon if you'd like.

I wish for you that every time you walk
into a coffee shop somewhere (anywhere)
someone says, "Hey there, What do you know, Joe?"
and makes you smile and feel like you matter.

You are the ones who lavishly give to your customers.
To someone like me. Just because.
You hot tickets. You eclectic bunch. You Major Dickasons
behind the counter.
You blessings before my eyes.

I wish for you that when the story gets hard
all black coffee bitter, and bran muffin stale (as life can
sometimes be)
you will still be known as that good old guy or gal
with that friendly face.

Everyday, twice a day I arrive.
It's a ritual with me. The large non – fat Cafe au Lait.
I really like it.
But no. I'm not there for the caffeine.

I get my jolt for the day from you.
It's that simple.
So, I wish for you full satisfaction.
And every small generosity to come your way.
A life sweeter than the lone almond croissant left in the glass case
at three pm.
I wish for you everything you give to me when you pass me that
hot steaming cup.
Like how my heart feels...

All swollen and full.

Maya

She drags you into the poem easy
without hurting.

Speaks with honeyed richness

like black coffee
and a splash of bourbon.

Handcuffs you
to an easy chair just enough –

as words Calypso dance

off her tongue

and reek of love.

Emeril's Chowder

He makes love in front of millions –
to the onions
smothered in butter –

then mutters, *"oh yeah baby,"*
like it's just what he needs.

He crisps the bacon –
wipes his hands on his apron
Now, he's got things shakin'

He's slick
or so he thinks,
adding more garlic.

He eye kisses a woman
among the crowd,
throws in a handful of clams
and yells real loud...

BAM!

Spanx

The stretch, the heft
that ugly flesh
colored Lycra for your jiggle.

The twisting, the contorting
the squirming wriggle.

The feet, the no feet
getting them on is a feat.

The lumps, the bumps
the new squish
out of your pumps.

The waistband, the rubber
the casing for your blubber.

The control?
The panty, the power
the new look of the hour.

The flatness, the *assless*
what it *lacksness* ...
Not me, not Charo
Not today, not tomorrow.

We're supposed to wiggle.

A Sweet Ride

Summer wind blowing through my hair.

I ride for miles without a care.

I cross the bridge from where you live

and think about what I would give.

If the breeze were to lay me down

on the cool green of the moss covered ground.

And lying next to me I saw your smile

and we had a chance to be awhile.

Red Ink

I could write to you in the air

something they can't read

or hear.

A loving prayer of some kind

from just the smile of you.

Shivers up my spine smudging the lines –

with this ink of ours.

Perhaps

All those extra beats,

irregular or whatever.

Was my way of showing that our love is still growing.

That fast pace and that
fear on my face.

Perhaps,
was my way of affirming

       my ever burning passion.

And just possibly
it was me having a hard time, finding the perfect lines
to write you

another love poem

of our very own.

Lovely

The sky last night, lit
Fire red copper.
Made me think of you.
Rousing yet delicate.

Like my name
coming off your mouth.
Breathless against the air.

I could taste the sky last night.
September apple smooth.
Deep pink sweet.
Sweet as the inward smile on your lips
recalling our pleasure.

The sky last night had your voice.
A faint recollection of you.
A love thumbprint.
A touch, a dream
against the quiet dusk.

My mind has played the night's sky.
I am stunned by its beauty.

Task

Laundry again

it never ends.

Sorting white load, dark load

hot water, warm

then cold.

A labor of love I believe

        to fold,

and smooth the collar;

the cuff with my fingers,

the sleeves with my palm.

And tucked inside a chest pocket

        a hidden prayer,

a sacred calm

        just for them.

Moments In Time

I wanted that moment to last.

I wanted it to last way beyond Wednesday night.

Past the swirling smoke

and the talk of the pasta fagioli

I wanted it to last beyond the full moon.

And the pulse of Van Morrison's beat.

Past the silent words.

And the racing earth.

Past the dreamy stars

And that look in your eyes.

I wanted that moment to last so I'd never forget.

Longer than the ripe tomatoes.

And the scent of the summer herbs.

And linger longer than

the small glass of red wine.

I wanted that moment to last

farther than my arms could reach.

And out last the runner's high

and the longing in my heart

and a good hard cry.

Beyond the time that is now.

I just wanted that moment to last.

Strawberry Moon

*"part of you pours out of me
in these lines from time to time"*
– Joni Mitchell

I sometimes wish I could find the strawberry moon
to thank him for the truth.
For spreading across the sky like a fat peach;
bobbing beneath the altar –
and preaching
his quiet sermon.
Let me recall that night
when the sun was loving on the moon
that way.
Let me feel the urgency
in the lungs of those forgotten words
that came from somewhere else,
and meant something.
Something holy,
if only to the single star
hanging suspended in the black air
of the church.

One Half

Cute little
half moon.
Honey pie.
Sitting there.
In a purple sky.

Sweet little thing.
Curvy curve.
Itty bitty tidbit.
Adorable hors d'oeuvre.

Pretty little baby.
White cream puffy.
On this quiet night
Oh so lovely.

Full moon.
What's all the fuss?
Cute little half moon.

You're just enough.

My Moon

I suppose the moon may even
get a bit lonely up there at times.
Moseying about the seas
in spite of the stars.
Insecure of his reflection
and the audience he has.

He too, is probably unsure
of his purpose in this world
or just how comforting
he is to look at.

Waxing Gibbous

dear muse
ignore
the bulge you see in
the moon tonight.

after all,
it's only a phase.
and nothing,
nothing stays the same.

The Same Moon

Do you see the same moon as I?
That lingers high
by night or day
in autumn's sight
and wonder why?

Or in summer's warmth
under sterling stars
this nighttime wondering,
is it ours?

Do you see the same moon as I?
That lies in fiery skies
among palettes red,
and wades away in winter's chill
with dreams of me still?

Do you see the same moon as I?
That saunters in when spring arrives
and flowers creep
from under?

For me I'll keep this eternal wonder.

Sorry

I didn't mean to.
But
I swallowed the moon last night.

I couldn't help myself.

I only wanted a kiss.

But
his lips
were all plump and sugary.

Buttery

....utterly

lovely.

He was a marshmallow
fellow.

And I
was really hungry.

Sorry.

The Moon and Me

I've been paying attention to the moon again.

I love how it borrows violet from the blue black of the night.

And once in awhile I throw on a sweater

and climb way up there. Behind the vastness, that spacious sky.

It's easier to breathe up there.

My hair eases down around my shoulders,

and suddenly there's a gentleness in my world.

And the moon, he holds my face in his hands.

And tells me he's never been loved this tender before.

I say I understand because it feels so good to feel so right.

And when I lean over and whisper in his ear I tell
    him everything.

He doesn't gossip to the stars or wink at the sun.

It's just me and him.

This Night Moon

I do not know what loving message
the moon keeps trying to tell me.
His face translucent, splayed out into the silence of the night.
I'm addicted to it whatever it is –
Sometimes it seems the only thing on earth without doubt
    or answers –
the one thing that is completely pleased with the world, and
thankfully says so.
I admire that about the moon.
And I wait in the blue hour
in the far away noise of the air,
hold my breath
reach up, and onto a white page, place him in my poem.

Spring

We wander lost in the streets of our first crush.
Where pretty pinks and yellows heave
and break ground like a sigh of relief.
And want as much as we do
to believe in a better world,
in a season that comes when called.

Everything and everyone seemingly
surrenders to this love.
This infatuation.
It's impossible not to want.

The garden quickens,
just like our hearts.
And we lean in
to kiss spring on the mouth.

Meditation

How kind of my body to remember me
she took me back so willingly.

My arms release to the bluest sky.
The birdsong and the day moon, outside.

My breath, a calming
A dawning of first light.

My thoughts blow away with the wind, and
Nothing beside me but the
sugary smell of spring.

Fresh Spring Peas

Six shiny bald heads tightly wrapped.

Sit snug
in a green kayak.

Little sailors front to back
giggle and sing yakety-yak!

Green pearls neatly strung.

One quick zipper pull

one happy tongue!

So Many Words

I can never find a pen
when you come to mind.
Words tangle and tease.
Vague above me.

It's your skin I need to pen down.
Like a verse on flesh.

The musk.
The sweetness.
The air of you on me.
Like a blessing.

How it turns into something beautiful
with my mouth.

Filling this white page
with slow murmurings
would be easy.

Bringing my soul forward.
Like the first light of morning unfolding.

Wet.

Just about
coming into flower.
My skin softer than what it was.
I can't be near enough
to you.

Where's the damn pen?

Love All Around
after the poetry reading

I want to reach out and hold onto my friends
awhile longer,
in the gentle clarity
of this blue sky.

I want to hold onto this feeling.
This lovely high.
In my heart
and in my life!

You Loving Me

You carefully, drew me a heart
On the misty window
Of my soul
How delicate it was
With its sweet curvy sides

And I watched it, as it set
And I embraced it
And never, has it melted
Or faintly, dripped away

You softly, blew me a forever
Like a kiss, off fingertips
Into my heart
How powerful it was
With its eternal promise

And I have lived this love
And I have cherished it
And I know for certain
It will always be.

Love Letters

I could read the sparkle in his I's
when he gazed in mine
and the L that rolled off his tongue
onto me
was no surprise
and how the O made me so aware
it was honey sweet
and so sincere
Oh please...
but when I heard him say the V
and he got up the courage to say the
E...
I just knew
YOU
were the one
for me.

This Kind Of Lightness

How the moonlight shone
that night,
casting off its shadows on us.

I lay on the floor
raw to the bone
as hungry lips ravage my body.

We are dizzying among
faint clouds
and warm smiles.

Lips knowingly say nothing.
Perhaps a silent whisper.
But in the heart and soul
a love exists.

The steady mist of light
slowly fades upon us
and into us.

We are submerged in each other
under this kind of lightness.

Inside My Heart

I close my eyes and it's all so clear

violins play music fills the air.

And there's a smile inside my heart

and I'm breathing love,

like the late day sun

and a taste of honey

your supple kiss a tingle, a rush.

And I'm happy when I close my eyes

for bells ring sweet, and you hold my heart.

And all is true in this world

of me and you.

Even tears taste of sugar.

Little Facts About Me

Skies at nightfall
and a farmhouse on a hill
make me cry
I don't know why.

I have late night conversations
with the moon
he tells me all about the stars
and I tell him about you.

You with your heart
magenta with love
all for me.

I like simple things
genuine people
and raw poetry.

I like your lips kissing
my forehead,
laugh lines
and imperfections.

We aren't perfect
but we are for each other.

Take Hold Of Me

I think about your thighs.
Their perfect curves and lines.

Their warmth
their softness,
a bit of lovely roughness
against mine.

Oh how I approve
how they move and slide,
take hold of me
and push mine aside.

Allure

There was just small talk involved at first.
With our eyes.

A pint of strawberries
uncut on the counter.

Fleshy and ripe,
like the swollen cheeks
of giggling school girls.

Through the window
the morning sun had found us,
and splashed sugar
over our skin.

It was strange how loud
the berries were calling.

You Tell Me

What could be more

intriguing than

one ripe, heavy red tomato

pressed up

against the mouth and

dribbling down a bit

                    over the curve

on the tan skinned chin

of the right man?

Real

And what if I had simply passed you by –
and missed eyes
that darkened with kindness.
A heart, that gathered light off my smile.
Or a mouth that spoke words
fulfilling me.

Those who have not loved you
will never know differently.

It's sad to think I might have missed that or
to have never known the certainty of it.

Fever

Every night
I look for you
in the sky.

Waiting here
with my eyes
and my mouth
and the milky ways of my thighs.

I'm so ravenous for the
moon of you
and the way you touch
the stars in me.

Like a blaze.

Without Words

Idle Time
You're all I ever knew of love
idle time
like a string tied to my soul
pulling me away
meticulous and beatific
driving a poem
through my heart
you're all I ever knew of love
— John Hardesty

A smile fell between us.

Sweetly.

A chance meeting of mouth and breath.

I took it home and cupped it
to my chest.

It was lovely and warm.

This gift given freely.

Purely unasked for
by a heart.

I love so hard.

Ode To Welles

To you who gives so freely

of flesh and breath and love.

To you who trusts so tender

with eyes and ears and self.

To you who fills my mind

with words not invented yet.

To you to you

who lush my heart.

Who lets me lose myself

and tuck a poem

in the sweet curve of your neck;

I adore you.

I Whisper To Ford

tiny body perfect
tell me what you are dreaming –
your shoulders at rest

do you hear the bird song
in the blue branches of this world?

or are you floating
over silent waters like a meditation
breathing this way and that way

how great your energy
how humble your effort
so kind, so delicate

your thoughts, uncomplicated
as light and airy as moths
flitting about the moonlight –

pure soul,
tell me what you know
that most have forgotten

let us in on your silence
your stillness
into something better;
a prayer, a secret

your own little
precious poem.

Baby Love
(after reading Mary Oliver)

I do not know what precious things
the baby keeps saying to me.

His voice easing out of his throat,
his mouth, his body,
into the air
of the early morning.

I like it
whatever it is.

I like his little applesauce breath.

I like the sweetness of his vowels,
his consonants; raw and untrained
spilling into my heart.

I imagine he is saying "there couldn't be a more splendid world
and here I am existing in it."

One Sunny Fall Morning

I stop writing a poem to pray.

Poem words can wait.

On the way to the patio door

I leave a few verbs; the actions I need to walk outside.

Laying similes on the steps like a flower girl

I look up and hang a string of pillowy metaphors by the cloud line.

I see the inside of my heart full with the ones I love.

In my mind God is smiling.

I'll get back to the poem later.

I'll get back to being a woman.

But for now there are these little folded hands

and somewhere a small girl

kneeling next to her mother

by the side of the bed.

Watching to see how it's done.

Free

Wings could save me some days.

 Days when life gets me down.

When I'm oh so weary

and every single minute seems so dreary.

Wings could make my spirits soar.

I'd glide so high into a purple sky.

Up past the trees and the cottony clouds,

I'd drift away from the bustling crowds.

All by myself so peaceful I'd be.

Wings could help me.

Be free!

One Night of Comfort

One night as I lay sleeping
soft winds blew across my face
like a brand new day
in the middle of the night.

One night as I lay sleeping
the sun rose in my heart
and my whole body felt
like one glorious smile.

One night as I lay sleeping
a petal from a beautiful flower
opened up and invited me in
and I drifted into the sweet nectar.

One night as I lay sleeping
I remembered the wind,
the sun and the flower,
and I knew God was holding me.

Ode to a Christmas Tree

I
want to
be chosen at the farm.
cut down, dragged and netted
thrown high on a station wagon
and go for a ride and feel the icy breeze
on my limbs only to thaw soon in a living room.
I want help standing up since I can't stand on my own
I want to smell real good and be doused in lights
the fat, colored ones
and strings of popcorn and cranberries hung, around
and around and around me and tinsel. I want tinsel.
I don't want to be forgotten. I want someone to
write

a

poem

about

me.

Big Red Love

An affair to remember and rekindle each year
the love apple of the garden my juicy red sphere.

Sun kissed flavor so sweet and robust
it feels just like love but maybe it's lust.

My mind you fascinate paired with basil you dance
I can't help but revisit this sultry romance.

Plucked straight from the vine drawn up to my face
my teeth ache to seize this fancy orb of such grace.

One bite punctures and bombards me with juice
I knew it was coming such carnal abuse.

Slippery seeds expelling all around my face
no chance of capturing them scattered all over the place.

The tomato the Pomodoro the Lypocene King
a tender brief indulgence my summertime fling.

Pine

I feel sorry for the tree
and the viburnum that sat next to it.
Its frail white clusters weeping
from the loss.
The air between them, gone.
I think I know how she feels.

There's a bashful white lilac who
stood in the background all these years.
You'd cry if you could see her.
She is grieving in the quiet unfamiliar,
and bent over
holding her heart.

On the other side stands the rhody.
He's pretending to be as strong
as the deep purple
he bears.
The leaves have gone brownish black
and are beginning to curl.
It's not even midsummer.

I wonder if he'll ever recover.

A few feet away from the trauma;
stands a tender pink dogwood –
from a seed I imagine, carried
from a bird's mouth one day.
It stands as round and wobbly
as a child would draw it.
It doesn't know what to make of all this.

I wish I knew.

Farmers Market

Vegetable avenue. The smell of dirt and the fresh earth.
And nothing, nothing but clean food.
Ruddy faced beets and greens and deep purples.
As raw and ripe as newborns in their cradles.

Potatoes, an entire mob scene.
Tomatoes, hysteria among fingers. Groping,
and hoping to cop a feel.

Sunflowers with smiles on their faces.
Huddled up beside the corn.
Fit to bust.
Accommodating themselves to the wooden crate.

Dark skinned figs. Split open.
Flirting.
Luring me in with their evocative flesh.
I was just passing by. They must want me.

Butternut squash. Hard.
As orange as the sky now.
Cuddled beside a blanket of chard.

Mushrooms. Wild as my mind at all this.
Why would I ever want to leave here?

The pears and the apples.
Sugar by the mouthful.
Heaving and breathing out loud.

Pumpkins of all kinds rich and warm.
Glowing. Already lit from within.

Hoards of berries.
Golden, black and blue.
Juice on the balls of my thumbs.
Love on my mouth and my tongue.

And then honey.
Sweet lovefest.
Summer's gift from the bees.

Tasting Notes

I think I detect my dad's left handed
broken-in baseball glove – black leather
from 1944 when he was drafted by the Yankees
farm team in upstate NY.
        Playing summer baseball in the street, I'd
press it to my nose,
           breathe it in –
           feel comforted and wait for a fly ball.

I swear I smell tobacco
from my grandfather's Camel non filters
as I buried my face into his brown woolen
sweater, as he hugged me hello
        stepping out of his car in 1960 –
Driving all the way from New Jersey to see us.

 And there it is — ripe black raspberries from my
cousin's backyard.
        Scraggly bushes along the fence.
        Our thumbs and lips stained blue and
thorn bloody.

Finally and forever I am aware of the figs on my
tongue
from that winter kiss standing in the kitchen –
          my heart racing,
          sweet caramelization, sweet
caramelization, dammit.

Thank you God for all that. And wine.
So alive and breathing still.
The fullness.
Swallowing the December moon.

Lips

Yours are so perfect,
pink and not too thin
but full enough.
a rosebud mouth
like my mother called it when she talked about mine as a baby.

I think of your lips
arriving at my neck, lost in my hair
when you called me baby –
how your breath was always sweet
like the insides of roses;

roses.
and then
rose
        petals,
    falling
purely
over my shoulders
my breasts
my torso
where you buried yourself in a field of them
and made me a whole raft of roses,
kneeling;
and took me away
over the sea to an island
we'd escaped to.

Writer's Block

Idle brain
Everything vague
Inane.

Empty matter
Hopeless chatter
Dismal pattern.

Barren noodle
The whole kit and caboodle
Futile.

Think tank
Nothing in the bank.
Angst!

Farmhouse

But what I'm really imagining is Iowa.
Acre upon acre of organic earth:
moist to my touch

and our house coddled under miles
of cotton clouds and sky

and sheets on the line
the wind blowing them easily
like sip between sip of oolong tea

the chestnut colored cow taking his sweet time
roaming the pasture
as I pick wild greens for dinner

and the cute chicken coop
with just enough eggs
I gather in the hem of my apron

a ladder in the old barn propped up
against the loft
making the moon and dreams reachable

and you and me and a drowsy song on the radio
slow dancing in the kitchen

Boy Humor or God We Love Our Boys

I want you both to know
you always make us happy.
Always.

But what made us happy that time during
                    lunch at Tulia,
  – our bellies filled to the brim with caponata
when we were all laughing hysterically about the
Whole Foods butcher –

"Dan, It's happening again ...
the chicken is smelling ..."

my sides hurt;
and none of us could catch our breath.

And then dad said, *can we beat a dead horse anymore?*
that practically killed us ...

During Mi Mancherai

Before the violin
gave way
and let her chestnut hair down,
things were as they have always been.
The sky, like the sea
a cold blue of endless.
The moon a mere face in the night.

Now, when she wails
into the chaos of the song;
east of him, west of him
she draws the bow across my heart.
My world, a hectic red ripe.
Tears autumn orange
scuttle and scald my face.
My face that's pressed
once again upon yours.

When did the sky and the sea
become reachable...
The moon generous, touching my hand?
Listen.
I remember this sound.
Keep the evening over us.

Dr. M.

Nowadays, when I wake –
it's you I think of.
I see your smile,
shining like a soft light
from deep inside you.

I remember your humble way
and confidence
in answering my fears.

Slowly, your faith grew into
my courage.
So, instead of backing away,
I handed you my heart.
And you knocked
the hornets nest away
and stopped the marathons.

These days.
It's you first thing
in the morning.
I pray.
I wish you well.
I thank you.

And just so you know,
I carry your smile and faith inside –
like I carry steady blessings for my children
my dad's laugh
the red lungs of a sunset
and the way the harvest moon
carries autumn.

When We Die

Let's suppose when it happens and we close our eyes,
we hear Bach's Suite No. 3 in D Major.
And our body is limber and lovely and light.
As light as a feather but floating upward this time.
And everything you feel is warm like a newborn baby sound
asleep lying on your chest.
And there are so many flowers, so many –
and each one opens up,
and inside each flower you see them, the people you have missed
and they are smiling like before.
And you look around and there are all the dogs you've ever
known romping around together. And you whistle and their ears
perk up because they now know, and you call all their names and
they come running and it's crazy. You say to them, "this is crazy!"

An old friend of yours is leaning against a peach tree. The juice
from the peach he is eating is dribbling down his happy to see
you mouth.
He tosses you one, you catch it effortlessly. One bite has you
saying, "best peach I ever ate".

Every piece of your once broken heart isn't broken anymore.

And it's great cuz you get a second chance to catch that fly ball
you missed and another chance to thank that someone who you
meant to thank.

And in the kitchen is your momma. She's waiting for you at the table with a bowl of steaming al dente rigatoni with the red sauce that you loved so much. And a piece of bread to sop it all up, from that round crusty loaf.

And your heart is literally on your sleeve and all the ones you have loved are inside it.
You want to touch everyone, touch everything –
and you can and you do!

And even though you couldn't sing well back then,
now you are singing.
And everyone is singing with you. And there are guitars
and pianos and violins and you might have cried before but now you don't because, well you just don't.
Everything is beautiful and happy and this is what it's like but no one told us.
How could they?
And all your imagined forevers are here in this soothing place.

There are no unanswered questions anymore.
And you don't even question that.
You can touch the stars and hear everyone's wishes. You even see a few of yours in there.
There are so many best parts coming to you from all your practiced shows of faith.
Everything is turning out the way you'd like.
It's no small thing you've been in line for –
this place right beside the full moon.

Kiss

Your sweet butter kiss

left a poem in my mouth

and that's why I write.

About the Author

Linda Recco O'Connell grew up in the 1950s in Needham, Massachusetts into a hardworking retail family business. She attended college in upstate New York and soon returned to join her father in his wine business. After her marriage, family life became her focus as she raised two boys. Motherhood was saddened by several miscarriages, and it was these painful experiences that inspired her to begin expressing herself through poetry.

Her poems have appeared in a number of journals, including *Soul-lit, SheMom, A Year of Being Here,* and *Wellesley Weston Magazine.* Her poem "Reunion" was presented as the basis for a song, as part of a London musical.

O'Connell resides in Wellesley, Massachusetts with her husband, Mike.

Writing My Way Home is her first book.

To learn more about her poetry, please visit:
www.facebook.com/LindaReccoOConnellPoetry